Medieval Illuminated Manuscripts

Coloring book

A journey into the Middle Ages

Nester Lethbridge

This book belongs to

_____

The Medieval era was a world that left one of its more fascinating records in illuminated manuscripts. Before the invention of the printing-press, a book was a hand-made work of art, a labor of love and patience decorated with countless miniatures.

This coloring book will take you on a journey through an assorted selection of 30 illustrations from authentic illuminated manuscripts, featuring scenes whose subject matter ranges from the joys and sorrows of everyday life to the celestial heights of sacred visions.

Now it's time to enjoy and bring the wonders of this bygone era to color and life.

Liberacio sponse.

Plog᷑ sci beronimi pbr̄m. in

ST. MATHEX

Sons g̃cis noniub'

.HILDEBERT.

mensa hildebṙi.

.everwinus.

Gottes sun hat ereret victores gottes frent · David · Osee xiij
h. O mors ero mors

v9 Signas te criste: golyā g'terit iste

Zachā. ix. | Vir sāgnīe tedāy et tu e nultū victos | Genesi xlix.

v9 Sic cristi morte. fit al' destructio portae

Prondens animas

Ducade thesauro

SO
THY

desponsatio sponse

deceptio sponse

latro

Printed by Amazon Italia Logistica S.r.l.
Torrazza Piemonte (TO), Italy